Unsung Heroes

Pioneers in Science

Elise Wallace

Publishing Credits

Rachelle Cracchiolo, M.S.Ed., *Publisher*
Conni Medina, M.A.Ed., *Managing Editor*
Nika Fabienke, Ed.D., *Series Developer*
June Kikuchi, *Content Director*
John Leach, *Assistant Editor*
Courtney Roberson, *Senior Graphic Designer*

The TIME logo is a registered trademark of TIME Inc. Used under license.

Image Credits: pp.6–7, p.8, p.9, p.39 (bottom) NASA; p.10 Kris Connor/WireImage; p.11 Kathy Hutchins/Shutterstock; p.13 North Wind Picture Archives/Alamy; p.15 (top) Royal Astronomical Society/Science Source; p.15 (bottom), p.18, p.21, p.23 Science History Images/Alamy; p.17 Francis Miller/The LIFE Picture Collection/Getty Images; p.22 Pictorial Press Ltd/Alamy; p.26 Library of Congress [LC-USZ62-131541]; pp.28–29 Ann Zane Shanks/Science Source; p.31 B Christophe/Alamy; p.32 Science Source; p.36 (bottom) Photo by Stuart-Rodgers Photographers, courtesy of Skidmore, Owing & Merrill LLP; p.37 Songquan Deng/Shutterstock; p.38 (top) Library of Congress [LC-DIG-highsm-09905]; p.38 (second from top), p.41 public domain; p.39 (top) Everett Collection Inc/Alamy; p.40 Library of Congress [LC-USZ62-131540]; all other images from iStock and/or Shutterstock.

All companies and products mentioned in this book are registered trademarks of their respective owners or developers and are used in this book strictly for editorial purposes; no commercial claim to their use is made by the author or the publisher.

Library of Congress Cataloging-in-Publication Data
Names: Wallace, Elise, author.
Title: Unsung heroes : pioneers in science / Elise Wallace.
Other titles: Pioneers in science
Description: Huntington Beach, CA : Teacher Created Materials, [2018] | Audience: Grades 7 to 8. | Includes index.
Identifiers: LCCN 2017056436 (print) | LCCN 2017058372 (ebook) | ISBN 9781425854775 (e-book) | ISBN 9781425850012 (pbk.)
Subjects: LCSH: African American scientists--Biography--Juvenile literature.
  | Women scientists--Biography--Juvenile literature. | Prejudices--Juvenile
  literature. | CYAC: Scientists--Biography.
Classification: LCC Q141 (ebook) | LCC Q141 .W21195 2018 (print) | DDC 509.22--dc23
LC record available at https://lccn.loc.gov/2017056436

Teacher Created Materials
5301 Oceanus Drive
Huntington Beach, CA 92649-1030
www.tcmpub.com
ISBN 978-1-4258-5001-2

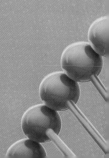

Table of Contents

Celebrating "New" Heroes

Some scientists are recognized by everyone. We have heard their names again and again. We know Isaac Newton and his three laws of motion. We have heard about Albert Einstein and his famous equation, $E = mc^2$. But what about Rosalind Franklin or Fazlur Khan (FAHZ-luhr KAHN)? Franklin was essential to the discovery of the structure of DNA, and Khan was a revolutionary **engineer** of skyscrapers. Yet their names are hardly known and rarely covered in history books.

For the scientists featured in this book, recognition was difficult to obtain. Even attempting careers in their chosen fields, whether astronomy or engineering, was an uphill battle. But these unsung heroes kept fighting. They refused to be held back by the prejudice of others.

Each inventor in this book made great contributions to his or her field. Though they made their discoveries decades ago, many will likely be new to you. So, let's celebrate these "new" heroes of science!

Brilliant Botanist

Ynes Mexia was a Mexican American botanist. Born in 1870, she was an avid explorer. She traveled the world, studying and collecting plants. During her life, she discovered over 500 plant species!

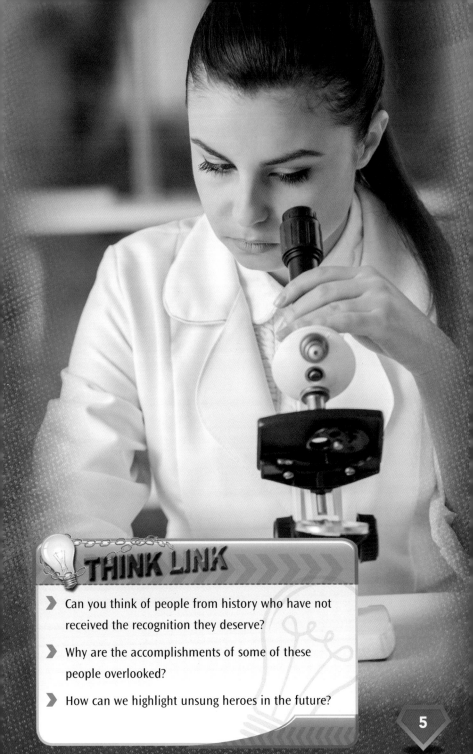

THINK LINK

> Can you think of people from history who have not received the recognition they deserve?

> Why are the accomplishments of some of these people overlooked?

> How can we highlight unsung heroes in the future?

Beyond the Stars

In the 1950s and '60s, women supported NASA as mathematicians. They were not treated with respect. These women, called *computers*, were tasked with checking calculations. No matter their accomplishments, there was little chance of promotion, simply because of their **gender**. But they did not give up. These women made huge impacts in the field of astronomy, whether others liked it or not!

Katherine Johnson

Thanks to the success of the film *Hidden Figures*, Katherine Johnson's name has gained recognition. She was one of the computers who worked at NASA during its early years. But Johnson was so much more than that. She was responsible for calculating the **flight paths** of some of the most historic NASA missions.

Space Race

NASA stands for "National Aeronautics and Space Administration." It was established in the late 1950s, when the United States was competing with Russia. Each country was eager to be the first to put a man on the moon. Johnson was working at NASA during this exciting era.

Math Maven

Johnson was a math whiz from an early age. When she was just 10 years old, she began high school. She graduated from college at age 18!

Put My Name on It!

When Johnson began working for NASA, women's research and writing went **uncredited**. That changed in 1960, when Johnson became the first woman in her division to be listed as an author.

Johnson reviews her work.

Freedom 7 was the name of the first mission with a NASA astronaut—Alan Shepard—on board. Johnson plotted the spacecraft's flight path. She was not only the first female or the first African American to calculate such a mission, but she was the first person to ever do so!

The longer Johnson worked at NASA, the more her colleagues relied on her. She plotted the path of astronaut John Glenn's mission, named Friendship 7. This mission made history, making Glenn the first astronaut to **orbit** Earth. Johnson also calculated the path for Apollo 11, the first mission to send astronauts to the moon.

In many ways, Johnson's career was groundbreaking. She paved the way for other female scientists. Her brilliant work proved that women are essential in the sciences.

Separate and Unequal

Johnson and her African American colleagues worked at the National Advisory Committee for Aeronautics (NACA). They were part of the West Area Computing unit, which was **segregated**. They could not use the same bathrooms or dining rooms as their white coworkers.

The movie *Hidden Figures* shows the importance of celebrating the work of women and people of color. The film highlights the fact that the heroes of history were **diverse**.

The movie was a success, proving that there is a hunger for new kinds of stories. Nominated for many awards, the film was honored at the 2016 Academy Awards. There, *Hidden Figures* was in the running for Best Picture, Best Adapted Screenplay, and Best Supporting Actress.

Gold Medalist

In 2015, Johnson was awarded for her work with a Presidential Medal of Freedom. The medal is one of the highest honors in the United States.

Johnson and President Barack Obama

During the ceremony, the real Katherine Johnson appeared on stage with Taraji P. Henson, who played her in the film. Johnson was greeted with a standing ovation. Johnson said of the film, "It was well done. The three leading ladies did an excellent job of portraying us."

MEET THE WOMEN YOU DON'T KNOW,
BEHIND THE MISSION YOU DO.

HIDDEN FIGURES

Fellow Math Lovers

While in NACA's West Area, Johnson worked alongside two other legendary women. Their names were Dorothy Vaughan and Mary Jackson. Vaughan was a computer programmer, and Jackson was an **aerospace engineer**.

Caroline Herschel

Caroline Herschel was a British astronomer. She was born in the mid-eighteenth century. Her work is often overshadowed by that of her brother, Sir William Herschel. He was a royal astronomer who served King George III.

At first, Caroline followed the path of a musician. She performed as a singer at an English resort called Bath. Her brother played music as well. But before long, both turned their attention to the stars.

While living in Bath, William became interested in astronomy. He wanted to develop a new telescope that would be powerful enough to explore faraway stars. Caroline was his trusted assistant, recording his findings. But as William's work evolved, so did his sister's. She became crucial to his progress, while making extraordinary findings of her own.

A New Planet

William became famous when he discovered a new planet, Uranus (YUR-uh-nihs). It was the first planet to be found in thousands of years!

The Herschels explore the skies with a telescope.

Eye to the Sky

The Herschels were able to make their discoveries because of their powerful telescopes. These telescopes were unlike any of the time, and William made them by hand.

The Herschels were unique for their time. They explored the area outside of the solar system. Before, scientists did not know very much about objects outside of the solar system. But William's telescopes allowed them to look farther. They could look deep into space.

Once William began working for George III, Caroline insisted that she be paid as an assistant. The king agreed, and Caroline became one of the first women to be paid for scientific research.

Over years of research, she made many discoveries. She discovered comets, which are **celestial** objects made of ice and dust. She also discovered three **nebulae**—clouds of gas and dust in space.

After her brother's death, Caroline continued their work. She revised their research and cataloged thousands of nebulae. In 1828, she was awarded a gold medal for her work by the Royal Astronomical Society.

Silver Coin Galaxy

Among Caroline Herschel's many discoveries was the Silver Coin Galaxy (above). This bright galaxy earned its nickname from its coin-like shape. It is 11.5 million light-years from Earth.

I Spy a Comet!

Caroline was the first woman to discover a comet. She found eight in total. People of the time considered her a comet-hunter.

Caroline's notes and drawings of a comet

Chemistry Champs

Chemistry is the study of the building blocks of matter. Chemists, people who study chemistry, have discovered what the very air we breathe is made of! They have **manipulated** matter, combining **elements** to make new substances. The modern world has evolved around their findings, allowing us to live better *and* longer. But some of history's greatest chemists have not received proper credit.

Percy Julian

Percy Julian, a chemistry major, was a stand-out student. He graduated in 1920 at the head of his class. Even so, the odds of succeeding in his field were stacked against him. Julian faced extreme racial **bigotry**.

Despite his great record, Julian was rejected by many graduate schools. Finally, he was accepted by Harvard! Julian put his knowledge to good use. He became one of the most influential chemists of his time.

Fighting Fires with Foam

One of Julian's inventions was used in World War II. It was a foam that could put out fires. The foam was partially made of soy protein!

Breakthrough!

Julian is responsible for creating a drug called *physostigmine* (fye-zoh-STIHG-meen). The drug treats an eye disease called *glaucoma*, which can lead to blindness.

17

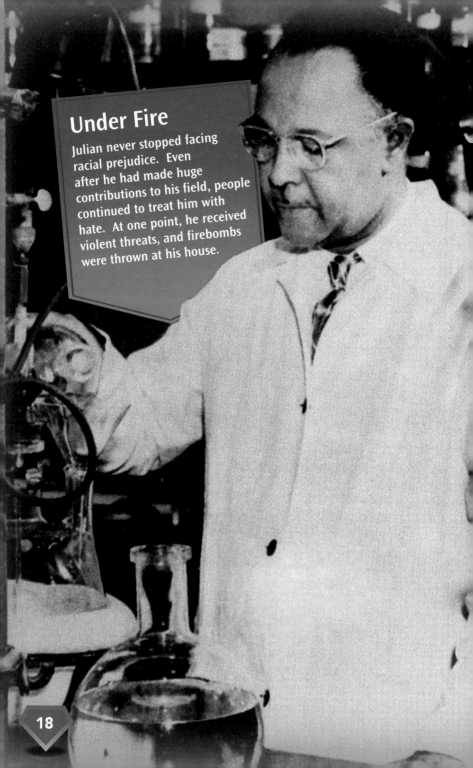

Under Fire

Julian never stopped facing racial prejudice. Even after he had made huge contributions to his field, people continued to treat him with hate. At one point, he received violent threats, and firebombs were thrown at his house.

Julian made many discoveries, often using soybeans. He used oil from soybean plants to make **hormones**, which are normally produced by the body. One of the hormones he made was **progesterone**. This hormone is used in some cancer treatments.

Julian's most famous success was creating cortisone in a lab. This **steroid** hormone helps treat inflammation. It reduces painful swelling in joints that comes with arthritis. It is also used to help with various skin issues, breathing problems, and other diseases. People all over the world benefit from the use of artificial cortisone.

The National Academy of Sciences later recognized Julian. He was one of the first African Americans to become a member. Still, few people know Julian's name. He is one of chemistry's great scientists.

Democracy in the Lab

Once he was an established chemist, Julian hired a diverse and **collaborative** team. He said, "We have a mixture of races and religions, and we work together and get along. If American democracy won't work anywhere else, we are determined to make it work here in our laboratory."

Rosalind Franklin

Rosalind Franklin was born in London in 1920. From the beginning, she knew she wanted to be a scientist. But even when Franklin was young, she was met with resistance. Her father didn't think women should attend college. Luckily, Franklin's aunt and her mother supported her passion for learning. In time, her father agreed, and Franklin studied at the University of Cambridge.

After graduating, she began to study the properties of coal. The fuel source was very important during World War II. Franklin's studies led her to key discoveries, such as the **microscopic** structure of coal. From this knowledge, Franklin categorized different types of coal and determined which would perform best.

Burning Questions

Franklin tested the properties of different coals by heating them to 1,112°F (600°C) and higher. She found that different coals had pores of different sizes and this affected how they burned.

lignite

anthracite

graphite

All for the Cause

During World War II, Franklin volunteered as an air-raid warden. During bombings, wardens helped the public. They directed people toward bomb shelters.

Franklin's most well-known work is her research into the structure of DNA. She used a unique method called **X-ray diffraction** to investigate DNA. Franklin used X-rays to look at **atoms**, the building blocks of matter. Atoms are so small that even with a microscope, people can't see them. Franklin developed a method using X-ray technology that allowed her to see the structure of different atoms. It was revolutionary!

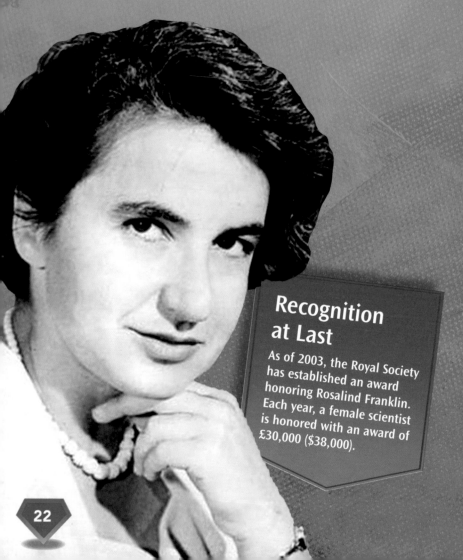

Recognition at Last

As of 2003, the Royal Society has established an award honoring Rosalind Franklin. Each year, a female scientist is honored with an award of £30,000 ($38,000).

Using X-ray diffraction, Franklin studied DNA. She discovered that DNA has a double helix structure. But Franklin was betrayed by one of her colleagues, Maurice Wilkins. Without her permission, he showed other scientists a photo that proved her great discovery. These scientists went on to win the Nobel Prize for discovering the structure of DNA. Franklin died without getting proper recognition for her work. But today, we celebrate her as a true genius.

Photo 51

Using X-rays, Franklin took a priceless picture. It showed the double helix structure of DNA. It is known as *Photo 51*.

Branches of Science

Science offers a variety of exciting career choices. Here are some specialized disciplines organized under the three main branches of science. What areas of study have not been listed below? In which branch or branches do they belong?

Physical Sciences

This science focuses on studying nonliving things. Scientists of this branch research everything from black holes to how to build bridges.

- astronomy
- chemistry
- physics
- engineering

Social Sciences

This science focuses on human behavior and culture. Scientists study topics such as communities, government, and economics.

- sociology
- political science
- economics
- anthropology

Life Sciences

This is also known as biological science, which focuses on living things. These scientists study flowers, animals, and other living things.

- biochemistry
- biomedicine
- botany
- zoology

Applied Science Stars

The applied sciences take what we know and put it to **practical** use. Some examples include medicine and engineering. The following scientists have made great contributions to their fields. All struggled to succeed, and all faced immense challenges.

Virginia Apgar

In many ways, Virginia Apgar broke the mold. Born in 1909, she was determined to succeed in the field of medicine. Initially, Apgar had planned on a career as a surgeon. She graduated from medical school and even completed an internship in surgery. But she soon found that her employment options were limited. It was the Great Depression. There were few jobs for surgeons, and they usually did not go to women.

Jane-of-All-Trades

From an early age, Apgar was known for her tireless enthusiasm. At Mount Holyoke College, she participated in many extracurricular activities. She acted on stage, competed in sports, and wrote for the college newspaper. Apgar even played violin!

Famously Fierce

Apgar was passionate about saving every life. She always kept **resuscitation** devices on hand, saying, "Nobody, but nobody, is going to stop breathing on me!"

Apgar tried something new. She focused her efforts on anesthesiology. This is the field of medicine that deals with **anesthesia** and its use, including resuscitation. It was a new and growing field. In the past, nurses dominated the field. But Apgar knew that some cases required a doctor's knowledge and experience.

Even so, being accepted into a training program was not easy. Apgar was denied admission several times. But at last, she was accepted! As Apgar studied, she became interested in the way anesthesia given to mothers affected babies during birth. During this time, she developed the Apgar score.

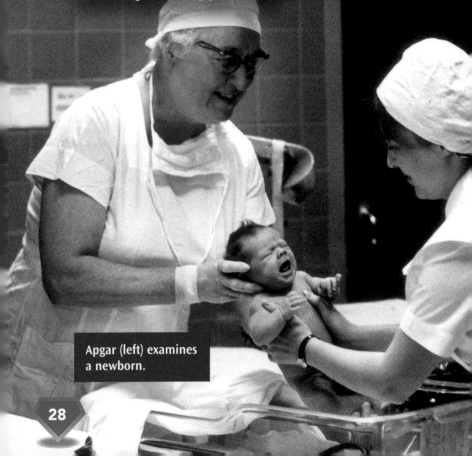

Apgar (left) examines a newborn.

The Apgar score is a method of checking the health of a newborn. According to the method, doctors must consider five different factors, including heart rate and breathing effort, when they inspect babies. They check them right after birth and again five minutes later. Today, Apgar's method is used by doctors all over the world.

STOP! THINK...

The Apgar score evaluates a newborn's health. Each category can have a score of 0, 1, or 2. The highest total score is 10. Look at the list below. What is the purpose of each category? Which of the categories do you think should be checked first? Why?

Activity
0 no activity
1 can move arms and legs
2 active

Pulse
0 no pulse
1 below 100 beats per minute
2 over 100 beats per minute

Grimace
0 no reflex irritability
1 some flexion of extremities
2 active motion

Appearance
0 blue, pale
1 pink body, blue extremities
2 pink

Respiration
0 no breathing
1 slow, uneven
2 vigorous cry

Charles Drew

Charles Drew grew up in Washington, DC. Born in 1904, he was raised in a racially segregated environment.

Drew would not have predicted his career as a scientist. As a child and during his teenage years, he had little interest in academics. He was popular and ambitious, but his focus was on sports—not school. In college, he was a sports superstar, playing football and running on the track team.

It wasn't until near the end of his college education that Drew turned his attention to medicine. Unfortunately, medical schools were segregated, and Drew, who was African American, had limited options. But Drew forged his own path. Eventually, he changed the world and became known as the "Father of the Blood Bank."

Boy About Town

Drew had a strong work ethic even as a kid. From a young age, he was earning money as a paper boy and lifeguard.

Motivated by Grief

After a long obsession with sports, Drew's interest turned to medicine. He was partly motivated by the death of his oldest sister. She died from tuberculosis when Drew was 16 years old.

At the time, blood was not stored in large quantities because it degrades, or breaks down, rapidly. Drew was able to develop a process for separating **blood plasma** from blood cells. This way, the plasma would last longer without refrigeration and not be destroyed during shipment across the ocean. His discovery was well timed. World War II was being fought, and many soldiers needed blood transfusions. Drew led the Blood for Britain project, which sent plasma to soldiers in the United Kingdom.

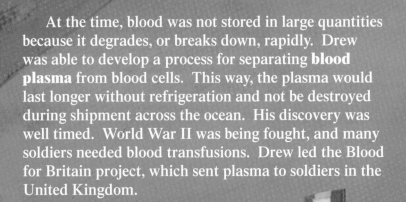

A Name to Last

A college in Los Angeles honors Drew. Its name is Charles R. Drew University of Medicine and Science. Since 1966, students have enrolled there study to become medical professionals.

Even at this stage in his life, Drew faced segregation. The American Red Cross didn't accept blood from African American people. Drew fought against this. Eventually, the Red Cross allowed African Americans to donate blood but still stored it separately. Drew wasn't able to convince them to end this practice. Drew's work saved many lives, both during the war and afterward.

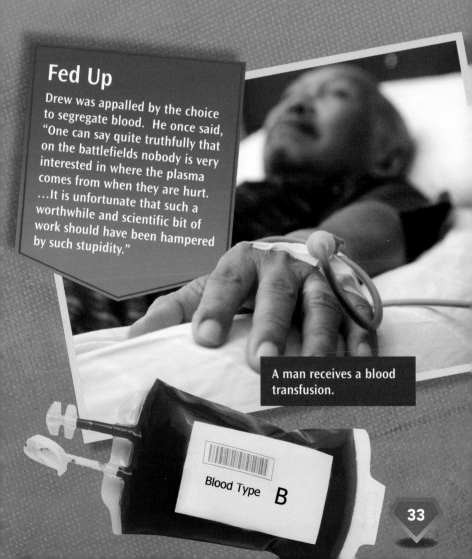

Fed Up

Drew was appalled by the choice to segregate blood. He once said, "One can say quite truthfully that on the battlefields nobody is very interested in where the plasma comes from when they are hurt. ...It is unfortunate that such a worthwhile and scientific bit of work should have been hampered by such stupidity."

A man receives a blood transfusion.

Blood Type B

Fazlur Khan

The engineering mind of Fazlur Khan was behind the design of some of the world's tallest buildings. Born in India, he made a name for himself by creating new ways to build structures. An inventive engineer, Khan is responsible for helping shape the modern skyline.

During college, Khan earned not one but *two* master's degrees. The first was in applied mechanics. This area of study centers on how objects respond to their environments. Thinking about how a building will respond to the forces of gravity is an example of applied mechanics. Khan's second degree was in structural engineering. This field relates to the designing and building of structures. Khan utilized both areas of knowledge in his biggest projects, such as the Sears Tower and the John Hancock Center.

Khan's Rule

Khan had high standards. He believed that "good architecture must also be good engineering and particularly good structure."

A Bold Building

Khan's John Hancock Center (left) was designed to stand out. The Chicago building is made out of imposing black steel.

Khan designed the Sears Tower, a project he was commissioned for in the early 1970s. Being selected for this project was a huge accomplishment. At the time, Sears was the biggest retailer in the United States, and the company wanted its headquarters in Chicago to reflect this status. Khan gave Sears exactly what it wanted.

The Sears Tower became an instant landmark. For over 20 years, it was the tallest building in the city. Khan developed a new structure for the skyscraper, called a *bundled system*. This system is both efficient and reliable. It uses a series of columns that look like tubes from the outside. Each tube is strong on its own, but together they are even stronger. Khan was the first to develop this system.

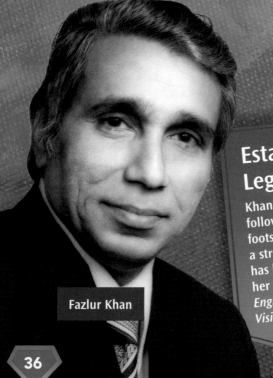

Fazlur Khan

Establishing His Legacy

Khan's daughter, Yasmin, followed in her father's footsteps. She, too, became a structural engineer. Yasmin has been central to preserving her father's legacy. She wrote *Engineering Architecture: The Vision of Fazlur R. Khan*.

New Name, Same Building

Today, the Sears Tower (right) is known as the Willis Tower. The building has 110 floors.

Unsung Heroes Through History

Take a look at the time line below. These are more of history's overlooked scientists. They come from every branch of science. How have their accomplishments impacted our world? What would the world be like without them?

Benjamin Banneker
African American scientist

Born in 1731

He was the first to build a clock in the United States.

Ada Lovelace
British mathematician

Born in 1815

She was the world's first computer programmer.

Carlos Juan Finlay
Cuban physician

Born in 1833

He proved that mosquitoes can carry and transmit yellow fever.

Lise Meitner
Austrian physicist

Born in 1878

She was crucial to the development of nuclear fission.

Rachel Carson
American biologist

Born in 1907

She was one of the world's first environmental writers.

Chien-Shiung Wu
Chinese American physicist

Born in 1912

She helped develop the atomic bomb.

Albert Baez
Mexican American physicist

Born in 1912

He created the X-ray reflection microscope.

Jocelyn Bell Burnell
British astronomer

Born in 1943

She discovered pulsars.

Ellen Ochoa
American astronaut

Born in 1958

She was the first Hispanic woman to travel in space.

Front and Center

You have met some "new" heroes of science, the men and women who worked against all odds to accomplish their goals. For many, the journey was long, difficult, and filled with obstacles. Some never received the recognition they were due, but all followed their passions for science and exploration.

The innovators in these pages have affected the world in many ways, from architecture to biology to astronomy. There are countless people in these fields and beyond who have been overlooked due to race and gender. And while the world has significantly improved in this respect, there is still much work to be done. If we want to make our heroes proud, we must continue pushing forward.

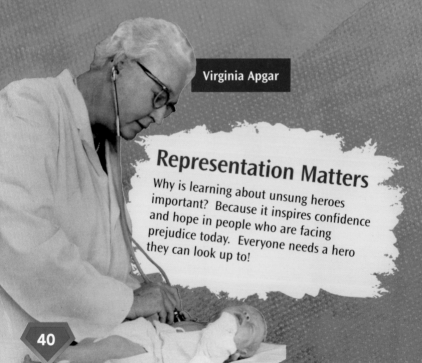

Virginia Apgar

Representation Matters

Why is learning about unsung heroes important? Because it inspires confidence and hope in people who are facing prejudice today. Everyone needs a hero they can look up to!

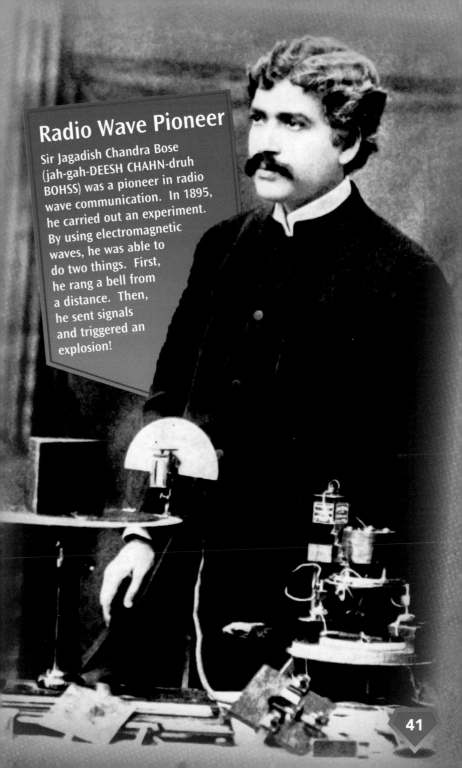

Radio Wave Pioneer

Sir Jagadish Chandra Bose (jah-gah-DEESH CHAHN-druh BOHSS) was a pioneer in radio wave communication. In 1895, he carried out an experiment. By using electromagnetic waves, he was able to do two things. First, he rang a bell from a distance. Then, he sent signals and triggered an explosion!

Glossary

aerospace engineer—someone trained in the field of engineering that deals with aircraft and spacecraft

anesthesia—the loss of feeling or consciousness through a substance

atoms—the smallest particles of a substance

bigotry—unfair acts or beliefs against people, ideas, etc.

blood plasma—a clear, yellow liquid that carries blood cells and other substances around the body

celestial—of or relating to the sky

collaborative—involving or done by two or more people working together to achieve something

diverse—made up of people or things that are different from one another

elements—basic substances that are made of atoms of only one kind and that cannot by separated by ordinary chemical means into simpler substances

engineer—a person who is trained to design and build complicated products, machines, systems, or structures

flight paths—the routes that an airplane or spaceship travels along through the air or space

gender—the traits typically associated with one sex

hormones—substances made and found in the body that influence growth

manipulated—used or changed something in a skillful way or for a particular purpose

microscopic—extremely small; able to be seen only through a microscope

nebulae—groups of stars that are very far away and look like a bright cloud at night

orbit—to travel around in a curved path

practical—relating to what is real rather than to what is possible or imagined

progesterone—a substance that occurs naturally in women and female animals

resuscitation—the process of bringing someone who is unconscious, not breathing, or close to death back to a conscious or active state again

segregated—separated by members of different races

steroid—a chemical compound that affects functions in the body

uncredited—not named or listed as one of the people who created something

X-ray diffraction—the spreading of X-rays

Index

Check It Out!

Books

Haber, Louis. 1992. *Black Pioneers of Science and Invention*. HMH Books for Young Readers.

Ignotofsky, Rachel. 2016. *Women in Science: 50 Fearless Pioneers Who Changed the World*. Ten Speed Press.

Shetterly, Margot Lee. 2016. *Hidden Figures: The American Dream and the Untold Story of the Black Women Mathematicians Who Helped Win the Space Race*. William Morrow.

Videos

Wall Street Journal. 2009. "Assigning an Apgar Score to Newborns." www.wsj.com.

Biography. "Charles Drew: Medical Pioneer." www.biography.com.

Websites

The White House: President Barack Obama. "The Untold History of Women in Science and Technology." obamawhitehouse.archives.gov/node/311241.

Biography. "Hispanic Scientists and Educators." www.biography.com/people/groups/hispanic-scientists-and-educators.

Try It!

You are creating a picture book focused on an unsung scientist. This scientist should be someone who is not highlighted in this book.

- Research your chosen scientist and his or her field of study. Think about the information you would like to pass on to the next generation. Choose 10 facts that you will illustrate in your picture book.

- Why was this scientist overlooked? What sort of struggles did he or she face?

- Your book should show what the scientist accomplished. How has his or her work changed the world?

- Write an outline of your book. Include sketches or copies of pictures. The book should be at least 10 pages long.

- Trade your outline with another student. Provide feedback.

- Using feedback from a classmate, rework the picture book until it's worthy of its unsung hero!

About the Author

Elise Wallace is the author of more than 10 books, including *Jurassic Classics: The Prehistoric Masters of Art* and *Spectacular Sports: Racing through Alaska.* She has written about world-record wildlife, bridges around the world, and the celebration of Día de los Muertos. Someday, she hopes to write a book exploring the life and work of Caroline Herschel.